The Author

John Chancellor has written biographies
of Charles Darwin, Richard Wagner,
John James Audubon and King Edward
I. He is also a publisher and antiquarian
bookseller. He is a keen gardener and has
a remarkable collection of early botanical
books which includes some of the flora of
the Holy Land. He has four children and
lives in London and New York.

The Illustrator

The watercolors were painted partly in
the Sudan and partly in Clifton, Bristol
in the 1880s by Lieutenant Colonel
William McCheane of the Royal Marine
Light Infantry. He was a friend of
Prince Louis of Battenberg and took
part in the Egyptian campaign of 1882
which ended in the defeat of Arabi
Pasha's forces at Tel-el-Kebir. He
completed these drawings in Clifton
after his retirement.

The Flowers and Fruits of the Bible

There is a lesson in each Flower,

A story in each Stream and bower,

In every herb on which you tread

Are written words, which rightly read

Will lead you from earth's fragrant sod,

To Hope, to Holiness, and God. *

David. *

THE FLOWERS AND FRUITS OF THE BIBLE

John Chancellor

Illustrated by

W. H. McCheane

BEAUFORT
BOOKS, INC.
New York

PLATE 1

A *Webb&Bower* BOOK

Edited, designed and produced by
Webb & Bower (Publishers) Limited
Exeter, England

United States edition published by
Beaufort Books, Inc.
New York, New York

Designed by Peter Wrigley

Copyright © John Chancellor 1982

Library of Congress Cataloging in Publication Data
81-69042

ISBN 0-8253-0085-1

Typeset in Great Britain by
MS Filmsetting Ltd, Frome, Somerset

Printed and bound in Hong Kong by
Mandarin Offset International Ltd

PLATE 1

And the Almond tree shall flourish,

Eccs Ch XII . Part of Verse. V .

PLATE 2

DEDICATION

*For Isabel, Katy and Anna—friends of flowers
and of the Scriptures!*

All thy garments smell of Myrrh, and Aloes, and Cassia,

Psalm. XLV. part of Ver VIII.

And God said, Let the earth bring forth grass, and herb yielding seed, and the fruit tree yielding fruit after his kind, whose seed is in itself, upon the earth: and it was so. And the earth brought forth grass, and herb yielding seed, after his kind, and the tree yielding fruit, whose seed was in itself, after his kind: And God saw that it was good. And the evening and the morning were the third day . . . And the Lord God planted a garden eastward in Eden; and there he put the man whom he had formed. And out of the ground made the Lord God to grow every tree that is pleasant to the sight, and good for food; the tree of life also in the midst of the garden, and the tree of knowledge of good and evil . . . And the Lord God took the man, and put him into the garden of Eden to dress it and to keep it. And the Lord God commanded the man, saying, Of every tree of the garden thou mayest freely eat: But of the tree of the knowledge of good and evil, thou shalt not eat of it: for in the day that thou eatest thereof thou shalt surely die . . . Now the serpent was more subtil than any beast of the field that the Lord God had made. And he said unto the woman Yea, hath God said, Ye shall not eat of every tree of the garden? And the woman said unto the serpent, We may eat of the fruit of the trees of the garden: But of the fruit of the tree which is in the midst of the garden, God hath said, Ye shall not eat of it, neither shall ye touch it, lest ye die. And the serpent said unto the woman, Ye shall not surely die: For God doth know that in the day ye eat thereof, then your eyes shall be opened, and ye shall be as gods, knowing good and evil. And when the woman saw that the tree was good for food, and that it was pleasant to the eyes, and a tree to be desired to make one wise, she took of the fruit thereof, and did eat, and gave also unto her husband with her; and he did eat.

(Genesis 1:11–13; 2:8, 9, 15–17; 3:1–7)

PLATE 3

A word fitly spoken is like Apples of gold in pictures of silver.

PR. Ch XXV. Ver XI.

INTRODUCTION

'Our researches into Nature are always attended with this happy effect; that the more we see of her works, whether animate or inanimate, the more we are convinced that the world, with all the vast variety of beings which it contains, is the work of an infinite and all powerful God.' This sentence is taken from a little book, published in 1826, on the literary and historical associations of those trees, plants and flowers which are mentioned in sacred and profane history. It is one of many books, written at about this time and later, which I have in my library, on the rewarding nature of the study of plants and other inhabitants of 'God's kingdom'. As the nineteenth century got into its stride, these books became more pious and Christian in character. The 'language of flowers' was a favourite subject for the brushes of young Victorian ladies; they chose to paint flowers exemplifying, so it was thought, Christian virtues of modesty, truthfulness, forbearance and so on. The drawing and the study of plants became part of a Christian education. *The Symbolism of Flowers, Flowers of Matins and Evensong*—these little books, with their delicate drawings and pious texts, made perfect presents at Christmas time.

The illustrator of this book, W. H. McCheane, was not a Victorian young lady but an officer in the British army. He did these drawings in the 1870s, when stationed in the Anglo-Egyptian Sudan. We may think of him after a gruelling day, spent keeping order among the infidel natives, repairing to the cool of his quarters, opening his Bible, taking out his paints and paint-brushes, and transporting himself to a world far removed from camp life in the tropics.

Although our artist was geographically much nearer Palestine and the plants of the Holy Land than the young ladies who drew similar subjects in their rectories, he was spiritually and artistically as much in England as they. His twin inspirations were the King James's Version of the Bible of the year 1611 and the flowers and fruits of English gardens. Where the Bible speaks of an apple, a lily or a rose, his thoughts turned to rose gardens, herbaceous borders and kitchen gardens in his own country and he drew the plants which would be growing there. We now know that the excellent authors of the King James's Version sometimes made mistakes when translating plant names from Hebrew or Greek into English; take, for example, the plants I have just mentioned—the Biblical 'apples', 'lilies' and 'roses' are, in fact, apricots, anemones and narcissi! How many of us knew that the fall of man was brought about not by an apple, but by an apricot? The Virgin probably never saw a white Madonna lily, without which any picture of the Annunciation is incomplete. There is no need, however, to follow too rigorously the dictates of botanical accuracy; let the archangel Gabriel continue to hold in triumph a *Lilium martagon* rather than an *Anemone coronaria*. Painting the wrong flowers will as surely lead us to God as painting the right ones. Many of the trees and plants which occur so often in the Bible—the olive, the fig tree, the grape vine and indeed 'lilies'—were part of daily household and country life in Palestine; our Lord deliberately brought them into His parables to make their meaning clearer to the simple people of Galilee. It is therefore spiritually, if not botanically, right for those who read the word of God, in Britain or in the United States, to see it manifest in the plants around them, even if these plants are not, as botanists say, 'indigenous' to the Holy Land.

Our artist must certainly have hoped that his beautiful watercolours would one day be published. Look at the exquisite pains he lavished on the title-page, each letter set in a sort of gossamer haze and on the illuminated poem by the young Irish poet Thomas Osborne Davis (1814–45):

> *There is a lesson in each flower,*
> *A story in each stream and bower,*
> *In every herb on which you tread*
> *Are written words, which rightly read*
> *Will lead you from earth's fragrant sod,*
> *To hope, to holiness, and God.*

His drawings and their illuminated captions from the Old and New Testaments should have the effect of turning us again to passages in the Bible which we have not read for many a year. Many of his quotations

Is there no Balm in Gilead? Jerⁱ Cⁿ VIII part of Vⁿ XXII.

They brought thee for a present horns of ivory and Ebony.

Ezⁱ Cⁿ XXVII part of Vⁿ XV.

are taken from the Song of Solomon, that most beautiful erotic poem which shows how much that great king fell a victim to sensual fantasies towards the end of his life.

The 'inaccuracy' of some of the artist's drawings will have, I hope, the happy double result of making us more familiar not only with the flower or fruit which he actually drew but also with that which he should have drawn. For example, the authors of the King James's Version translated a Hebrew word as 'mulberry' when it should have been 'poplar'. In my notes I describe the Hebrew 'mulberry' rather than the illustrated English mulberry. This happens on several occasions.

In this age of science and scholarship we cannot let ourselves be a party to the perpetuation of fallacies and inaccuracies. Art must be truthful; we cannot 'cover up' for our artist; we can enjoy his paintings as paintings, but we must discover at the same time the actual identity of the mistranslated plants. One way of doing this is to go to the Holy Land and look at the plant life for ourselves, as I did before writing this book. I shall return to this later.

It could be said that if plants, like other works of creation, are worthy of study, they are especially so when seen in connection with the Scriptures. Lack of knowledge of a certain plant may hide much of the force and beauty of a parable. 'Consider the lilies of the field' (Matthew 6:28) is a good example. When we know that it is the Palestine anemone or windflower which surpassed 'Solomon in all his glory', the meaning of the parable becomes more vivid. The anemone is a modest plant which covers the Holy Land in spring with its red profusion; the lily, on the other hand, is the kind of majestic plant which you might expect to be growing in the courtyards of a powerful and civilized king.

In the old days it hardly occurred to people that plants growing in one country did not necessarily grow in another. In England herbalists attempted to identify wayside plants which had been described in their native Greece by the early botanical 'fathers', such as Theophrastus and Dioscorides, in the first century BC. Until the eighteenth century interest in plants was mainly medicinal and superstitious; it was important to know, for example, which plants could best protect us from the spells of witches or the attacks of the pox. Immense authority was attached to the pronouncements of earlier writers. In no field was this attachment to authority stronger than in the study of the Bible.

Plants are referred to in many hundreds of pages in the Bible and theologians and scholars have been commenting freely on them for two thousand years. For a long time nobody dared to challenge any of the translations or Biblical interpretations by the leaders of the church then in authority. It goes without saying that these writers were not botanically trained and the points they were trying to make were more likely to be philosophical, moralistic or philological than botanical. Of course it never occurred to them to ask what plants were growing in the Holy Land in their day; in fact it never occurred to anyone to go to Palestine and look at the vegetation with his own eyes until Hasselquist, the pupil of the 'Immortal Swede' Linnaeus, went there in 1749. At the urging of his master, who had complained that less was known about the natural history of the Holy Land than that of India, this delicate young man spent two years in Egypt and Palestine, where he died of the excessive heat. Linnaeus arranged the posthumous publication of his book, *Iter palaestinum*, in 1757. This book began a new age in the study of Bible plants; for the first time a writer on the natural history of the Bible had actually visited the Holy Land and studied the plants of the area.

Botanists were very slow in following up the initiative of Hasselquist. For some reason or other, they preferred to botanize in Europe or in far more distant parts. Perhaps they were inhibited by some pious disinclination to treat scientifically those plants which grew on holy ground, like breaking in where angels fear to tread. Perhaps, as botanists, they were put off by the hybrid character of the area, being a botanical meeting place of three continents. Who knows? At any rate, it was some time before the

PLATE 5

I have seen the wicked in great power, and spreading himself like a green Bay tree.

Psm. XXXVII. Ver. XXXV.

misidentifications of the King James's and other versions were corrected. Aspens or poplars continued to be called 'mulberries', mulberries to be called 'sycamines', the acanthus to be called a 'nettle', the almond a 'hazel', the plane tree a 'chestnut' and the apricot an 'apple' for a long time to come.

W. H. McCheane's watercolours provided me with a welcome excuse to pay my first visit to the Holy Land. I flew on Easter Saturday from London to Tel Aviv and taxied to Jerusalem. My Iraqi driver could not find the Convent of the Sisters of Sion where I was to be staying. Instead he dropped me at a church in the village. It turned out to be the church of St John the Baptist, built on the spot where the saint was born. Now it was nearly midnight on Easter Eve; the taxi had gone and I stood in the yard in front of the church; a whiny sound of chanting came from within; the door of the church was ajar, so I crept in with my suitcases. Several old women carrying lighted candles turned around. The church was full; a young dark-haired priest said Mass in barely comprehensible French. He was a Spanish Franciscan. It was a spacious, domed, Renaissance-style church, the walls covered with varied blue patterned designs, apparently the gift of the Queen of Spain. The altar was decorated with arum lilies and hanging from the ceiling were florid gilt lanterns.

After Mass I walked to the hospice or convent with some of the Sisters, who insisted on helping to carry my suitcases. They belonged to the order of the Sisters of Sion, founded in the 1890s by Theodor Ratisbon and his brother. Both were Jews and came from Strasbourg. They wanted to bring together Christians and Jews in joint worship; an example of this is the singing of the psalms in Hebrew, which was in fact the whiny chanting noise I had heard as I stood outside the church of St John the Baptist. The English branch of the Sisters of Sion is established in the house of my brother-in-law in England, and this was why I came to stay with them in the pretty village of Ain Karem, the name meaning 'a spring'.

The convent is enclosed by castellated walls which reminded me of a crusader's castle. As I walked through the garden on that balmy Easter night I noticed palm trees and large clumps of rosemary and oleander (*Nerium oleander*), as outstanding a feature of the Holy Land as it is of Tuscany. Later I was to see many such thickets of oleander in the Jordan valley and elsewhere along water courses and wadis. '*Hearken unto me, ye holy children, and bud forth as a rose growing by the brook of the field*' (Ecclesiasticus 39:13). The 'rose' in Ecclesiasticus is thought to be the oleander.

Ain Karem, known in the Middle Ages as St John in the Mountains, and famous not only as the birthplace of John the Baptist but also for the shrine of the Visitation, has undergone a complete change of inhabitants since the creation of the State of Israel thirty-odd years ago. The 3,000 Moslems have been replaced by Jews. The monastic establishments and a handful of Christians remain. As I walked through the village at night during Easter week, noises came out of the houses in celebration of the Jewish *Pesah*, or Passover. The inhabitants would have been reading stories out of Exodus and eating at the same time bitter herbs and unleavened bread.

My bedroom in the convent had a view of dry hills where olives, vines and cypresses grew on rocky terraces. This was perhaps the country where the Baptist fasted on locusts and wild honey (Matthew 3:4). The faithful dislike the idea of the Baptist actually eating locusts; they prefer to think that he was eating 'St John's bread', the pods or carobs of the locust tree, *Ceratonia siliqua*. There is a fine locust tree in the convent garden; the pods taste like chocolate and are used in diabetic chocolate. I showed the watercolours reproduced in this book to Sister Marianne, and we walked through the convent's olive groves looking for wild flowers. I made a bunch of the following: camomiles, thistles, anemones, 'everlasting' (*Helichrysum*), poppies, broom, hyssop and chickweed (*Stellaria media*). The convent garden itself is laid out like an English garden with Mediterranean plants; in it you find palm, pines and cedars of Lebanon, lavender, geraniums, cacti, garlic, bamboos, mulberries, almonds, pomegranates, figs and Chinese lilac.

Ain Karem has a spring called the Fountain of the

PLATE 6

For of thorns men do not gather figs, nor of

a Bramble bush gather they grapes. Lu. VI ch Part of XLIV. ver.

Virgin, where she is said to have drawn water. She came here for her mystical meeting with Elizabeth and Zacharias, the parents of the Baptist. '*And Mary arose in those days, and went into the hill country with haste, into a city of Juda*' (Luke 1:39). Here she said 'My soul doth magnify the Lord' (Luke 1:46); here we are in the village of the *Magnificat* which is written in over fifty different languages on the wall outside the church of the Visitation.

In Jerusalem I rented a car and drove to Jericho, along the Jordan valley to the Sea of Galilee. Jericho, which Antony presented to Cleopatra and which Herod later acquired as a cool place in which to relax, is the oldest and most low-lying town in the world. It is an oasis in the desert and is surrounded by banana, date and orange plantations. Jericho first appears in the Bible with the arrival of Joshua and the Israelites on the other side of the Jordan. It was the 'city of palm trees' of Judges 1:16. Mark Antony gave it to Cleopatra because of its splendid gardens, whose palm groves and balsam trees were an important source of revenue. It was in a nearby cave that our Lord fasted forty days and forty nights after being baptized in the River Jordan. This was the finest hour in the history of that strange river, 233 miles long, which drops from the snows of Mount Hermon to the turbid depths of the Dead Sea.

A wonderful place from which to behold the Sea of Galilee is the Horns of Hattin, so called because of its two peaks which resemble horns. On the slopes of this extinct volcano the Crusaders suffered, on July 4th, 1187, a disastrous defeat. Here, within sight of the lake on which Jesus had walked, and under the burning heat of the sun, perished the Latin Kingdom of Jerusalem. 20,000 Christians fell for the sake of the Cross, and 30,000 were taken prisoner and later sold into slavery.

From the Horns of Hattin, then, we have a breathtaking view of the Sea of Galilee, a lake of changing moods, as we know from the Gospels—at times azure blue and motionless and at others dark green and sullen. I would like to have hired a boat and sailed, Gospel in hand, along the shores, stepping out at familiar places like Tiberias and Capernaeum. Instead I drove around in my rented motor car.

After lunching (on fish, oddly enough) at the restaurant of Loaves and Fishes, a few hundred yards away from Tabgha, where the multiplication of loaves and fishes took place, I drove up to the Mount of the Beatitudes and sat looking down to the north shore of the Sea of Galilee over the slopes carpeted in spring flowers—blue lupins, crimson anemones and red ranunculi. '*And seeing the multitudes, he went up into a mountain ... and he opened his mouth, and taught them, saying, Blessed are ...*' (Matthew 5:1–12). Our artist, McCheane, drew separately each of the beatitudes; the illuminated verses are surrounded by a frame of exquisitely drawn flowers; each beatitude has a different floral design. It was also, in all probability, on this spot that our Lord spoke the parable, '*Consider the lilies of the field, how they grow; they toil not, neither do they spin*' (Matthew 6:28).

There are many other wild flowers to be found around the lake and in other parts of Galilee—tulips, irises, crocuses, cyclamen, hyacinths, fritillaries, orchids, pinks, peonies, hellebores and snapdragons, to mention a few. The Sea of Galilee has a particularly warm climate, since it lies 655 feet beneath the Mediterranean. Orange trees flourish in Tiberias.

The hilly countryside of Galilee was covered with orchards and plantations—white flowering almonds (*Prunus amygdalus*); carob or locust trees (*Ceratonia siliqua*); redbuds or Judas-trees (*Cercis siliquastrum*) with their purple flowers appearing before the leaves and on one of which Judas Iscariot 'hanged himself' (Matthew 27:5); Kermes oaks (*Quercus calliprinos*) and Aleppo pines (*Pinus halepensis*), used for building the Temple. Weaving in and out of the trees were thistles, narcissi, wild tulips, daisies, cyclamen, anemones and clover.

Acre, or St John of Acre, has managed to keep its medieval appearance in spite of having been demolished stone by stone by the Mamelukes, who captured it on May 18th, 1291. Thus fell the last Christian stronghold in the Holy Land and with it the crusades came to an end. Life had not been pleasant

PLATE 7

Instead of the Brier shall come up the Myrtle tree.

ISAIAH. LV.ch part of XIII ver

for the Jews under the Latin Kingdom of Jerusalem; in the twelfth century they numbered barely one thousand in all Palestine and at the beginning of the thirteenth century there was only one Jew in Jerusalem!

From Acre we drove to the Dead Sea. Between the western shore and the arid mountains of the desert of Judaea are Qumran of Dead Sea Scrolls fame; Ain Gedi (fountain of the kid) where David hid from the wrath of Saul and where I saw my first 'Sodom apple' or 'Wild gourd' (*Citrullus colocynthis*), with its orange-like fruit, meant to be bitter and poisonous but tasting quite good to me; then Masada, Herod's mountain fortress, and finally Sodom, where nothing untoward was going on and Lot's wife could still be seen as a pillar of salt (Genesis 19:26). Further south crossing the desert from the Dead Sea to the Gulf of Aqaba and down into the Sinai Desert the only signs of life, apart from the occasional oasis of palm trees, where bedouins live with their camels, are the acacia trees (*Acacia tortilis*), called *shittim* in Hebrew. '*And he made the altar of burnt offering of* shittim *wood*' (Exodus 38:1). This attractive spreading tree is almost always mentioned in the Bible in connection with the Ark of the Tabernacle. These thorny trees were the only timber available in the desert. They and the occasional thorn bush provide the only splashes of green in its arid vastness. The wood is hard and close-grained and therefore suitable for tabernacle-making.

I hope this book will encourage you to set out for the Holy Land with a Bible in one hand and a botanical manual in the other.

PLATE 8

She took for him an ark of Bulrushes, and daubed it with slime and with pitch, and put the child therein, and she laid it in the Flags by the river's brink. Ex. Ch II. Ver III.

ALMOND *Prunus amygdalus (Rosaceae)*

'Also when they shall be afraid of that which is high, and fears shall be in the way, and the almond *tree shall flourish, and the grasshopper shall be a burden, and desire shall fail: because man goeth to his long home, and the mourners go about the streets'* (Ecclesiastes 12:5).

The almond tree (plate 1) blooms early in the year; in Palestine its pinkish blossoms may even be seen in January. Its Hebrew name *shaked* means 'waker'. For the Jews it was a 'wake-tree', a harbinger of spring, a reminder that winter was passing, that soon flowers would cover the earth and birds sing and the voice of the turtle-dove be heard once again in the land. Another Hebrew, and indeed Arabic, name for the almond was *luz*, which was sometimes incorrectly translated *hazel* (e.g. Genesis 30:37 *'And Jacob took him rods of green poplar, and of the hazel and chesnut tree ...'*). One theory is that *luz* refers to the tree and *shaked* to the fruit or nut; another that the former designates the wild tree and the latter the cultivated one.

The passage from Ecclesiastes, quoted above, suggests that the almond is a symbol of age and decay rather than of youth and spring. We must visualize a hoary-headed patriarch, whose hair is almond white, and whose active days are certainly over. Although almond flowers are pink, they give a snowy-white appearance when seen en masse from a distance. On the other hand, Jeremiah, when asked by the Lord 'What seest thou?' and answering, 'I see a rod of an almond tree' (Jeremiah 1:11) had in mind its regenerating, early flowering properties.

Aaron's rod is the most famous example of the miraculous budding of almond branches. '*...and, behold, the rod of Aaron for the house of Levi was budded, and brought forth buds, and bloomed blossoms, and yielded* almonds' (Numbers 17:8). It flowered and fruited overnight.

The almond tree flourished, it seems, in Canaan, notwithstanding the famines; that it did not grow in Egypt is suggested by the fact that Jacob sent Joseph a present of almonds: '*... carry down the man a present, a little balm, and a little honey, spices, and myrrh, nuts and* almonds (Genesis 43-11).

Almond trees were taken as models by the Israelites when designing golden candlesticks in the Sinai desert: *'And in the candlestick shall be four bowls made like unto* almonds ...' (Exodus 25:34).

The almond is closely related to the peach, nectarine and apricot. The latter is thought by some writers to be the apples of gold referred to in Proverbs (*'A word fitly spoken is like apples of gold in pictures of silver'* 25:11). It differs from them, of course, in having a soft husk which is not edible and which covers the kernel, its most useful part. Almonds have always been valued in the Near East for their oil. The Bible does not distinguish between sweet and bitter almonds; the bitter variety was more prevalent in the Holy Land.

ALOE *Aquilaria agallocha (Thymelaeaceae);*
Aloe barbadense (Liliaceae)

'All thy garments smell of myrrh, and aloes, *and cassia'* (Psalms 45:8).

'I have prepared my bed with myrrh, aloes, *and cinnamon'* (Psalms 7:17).

'Spikenard and saffron; calamus and cinnamon, with all trees of frankincense; myrrh and aloes, *with all the chief spices'* (Song of Solomon 4:14).

'*... and bought a mixture of myrrh and* aloes' (John 19:39).

The Old Testament 'aloes' (plate 2) are different from those mentioned in the New Testament in John 19:39. The former are a rare tree native to Assam and Burma and known as the lign-aloe or eaglewood (*Aquilaria agallocha*). Those of John are true or bitter aloes (*Aloe barbadense*). The lign-aloe has a heartwood known as agallochum; this is a soft and fragrant inner wood (quite different from the heartwood of ebony), used for incense, fumigation and also as a setting for precious stones.

The New Testament 'aloes' were used as a spice for embalming the dead; they have an unpleasant smell and a bitter taste. No wonder Nicodemus wanted to neutralize the smell with one hundred pounds of myrrh.

The true aloe is a handsome succulent plant; it has stiff fleshy leaves with sharp teeth which spring from a dense rosette just above the root. Its vermilion bell-shaped flowers, which appear early in spring, are carried on a single spike. The drug, aloin, comes from the pulp of the fleshy leaves.

PLATE 9

And the manna was as Coriander seed, Numᴮˢ Cʜ XI. part of Vᴱᴿ VII.

My beloved is unto me as a cluster of Camphire, Song of Solⁿ. Cʜ I. part of Vᴱᴿ XIV.

APPLES OF GOLD (apricot)

Prunus armenaica (Rosaceae)

'*A word fitly spoken is like* apples of gold *in pictures of silver*' (Proverbs 25:11).

The 'apple' of the Bible is not, in spite of the illustration (plate 3), our common apple, *Pyrus malus*. What it actually is has long been the subject of debate. The argument against the common apple is that it is not a native of Palestine; in the wild state its fruit was small and bitter and it would have taken many years of cultivation before it could begin to resemble the fruit described so glowingly by Old Testament writers.

Neither were Solomon's 'apples of gold' oranges. Although oranges are one of Palestine's main exports, they are not indigenous and, in fact, have not been there all that long. There were no oranges in Palestine at the time of Solomon.

Other candidates have been the citron (*Citrus medica*), which was ruled out owing to its bitter taste, and the quince (*Cydonia oblonga*), which fails to qualify for the same reason.

The apricot (*Prunus armenaica*) is now believed to be the 'apple' of the Bible. References to the 'apple' tree tell us that it offered shade, and that its fruits were sweet-tasting, fragrant, gold in colour and set in silvery leaves. This seems to point to the apricot, one of the most abundant fruits of the Holy Land.

'*As the* apple *tree among the trees of the wood, so is my beloved among the sons. I sat down under his shadow with great delight, and his fruit was sweet to my taste*' (Song of Solomon 2:3).

BALM (balsam) *Commiphora gileadensis* or

C. opobalsamum (Burseraceae)

'*Is there no* balm *in Gilead; is there no physician there? why then is not the health of the daughter of my people recovered?*' (Jeremiah 8:22).

'*Babylon is suddenly fallen and destroyed: howl for her; take* balm *for her pain, if so she may be healed*' (Jeremiah 51:8).

The Douai Bible of 1609 translated Jeremiah 8:22 as 'Is there no rosin in Galaad?' and the Bishops' Bible of 1568 as 'Is there no tryacle in Gilead?' These versions have ever since been known as the Rosin and Treacle Bibles.

The Hebrew word *tzori* referred to the liquid gum which flowed from a wounded balsam tree. The balm-of-Gilead tree was not, as its name implies, a native of Mount Gilead, which rises to a height of 900 feet above that portion of the Ghor Valley between the Sea of Galilee and the Dead Sea. It is indigenous to Arabia, particularly the mountainous regions of Yemen. From Arabia also came frankincense and myrrh. Balsam trees were cultivated in Palestine at the time of Solomon, particularly in the green oasis of Jericho. It is said that the Queen of Sheba brought the seeds as part of her gift of spices. '*And she gave the king ... of spices very great store, and precious stones: there came no more such abundance of spices as these which the queen of Sheba gave to king Solomon*' (I Kings 10:10).

The balm-of-Gilead tree (plate 4) is a small evergreen with straggling branches, trained like a vine. 'Balsam' or 'balm' is obtained from the stem, the fruit and the branches.

It has been suggested that Jeremiah's 'balm', which was essentially medicinal and not necessarily fragrant, was the Jericho balsam (*Balanites aegyptiaca*) found in the plains of Jericho and the rocky country of Gilead.

PLATE 10

And Jacob took him rods of

green poplar & of the hazel & Chesnut.

GENESIS. CH XXX part of VER XXXVII

BAY TREE *Laurus nobilis (Lauraceae)*

'I have seen the wicked in great power, and spreading himself like a green bay tree. *Yet he passed away, and, lo, he was not: yea, I sought him, but he could not be found'* (Psalms 37:35–36).

We have another example of a Hebrew word being given a different meaning by different translators. *Ezrach* of the Hebrew has been variously translated as cedar of Lebanon (*Cedrus libani*), oleander (*Nerium oleander*) and bay tree or true laurel (*Laurus nobilis*). Most authorities now agree that David had the bay tree, sweet bay, bay laurel or true laurel (all have the same meaning) in mind when he gave the 'green bay tree' as a symbol of prosperity (plate 5). It is, indeed, a matter of pride to possess a bay tree; there was one in my garden at Kew, a few steps from the kitchen. It could not claim to be a splendid example of its species, but its thick dark glossy leaves made it a comforting presence throughout the year. Travellers in the last century saw bay trees luxuriating in the old gardens of Tyre and Sidon and beside forgotten towers and deserted vineyards in the Holy Land.

Why did the bay tree symbolize for David complacency and affluence? It may have been its unchanging greenness and the aromatic fragrance of its leaves. The cedar of Lebanon is too majestic, and the oleander is, despite its glorious beauty, too profuse to denote exclusivity. The bay tree is neither majestic nor profuse; it can be found in woods and thickets from the coast to the foothills of the mountains. Although native to Palestine and growing around Hebron and Mount Carmel, it was never very common there. This may explain the one and only reference to it in the Bible; its pleasing appearance, refreshing shade and the agreeable odour of its leaves should have merited many a mention.

Apart from its thick glossy leaves, the bay tree has small, greenish-white flowers and berry-like fruits, the size of a small grape. The bay leaf has an unforgettable spicy fragrance and it is used throughout the world as a condiment. Its fruit, root, leaves and bark have always been used for medicinal purposes. The leaves also yield a green oil called 'oil of bay', not to be confused with the commercial oil used in making bay-rum.

In Greece and Rome bay or laurel leaves were used for crowning priests, poets, heroes and the victors of games. They crop up repeatedly in classical mythology. Daphne was turned into a bay tree by Apollo; its leaves gave oracles and soothsayers the power of prophecy; it kept away misfortune and protected a house from lightning.

The bay or laurel should not be confused with the garden laurel, i.e. the Portuguese laurel, which belongs to the same family as the almond and plum (*Rosaceae*).

BRAMBLE (elmleaf bramble) *Rubus ulmifolius (Rosaceae)*

'For every tree is known by his own fruit. For of thorns men do not gather figs, nor of a bramble bush *gather they grapes'* (Luke 6:44).

The bramble of the Holy Land is our good old blackberry bush (plate 6). There is little need to describe this prickly evergreen shrub which throws out its shoots in all directions. Among our earliest memories are staining our fingers on its juicy purple fruit or tripping over its treacherous suckers.

In Hebrew *atad* is translated as 'brambles' and as 'briers' and 'thorns'.

BRIER *Solanum incanum (Solanaceae)*

'Instead of the brier *shall come up the myrtle tree'* (Isaiah 55:13).

There are dozens of Hebrew words indicating a prickly or spiny plant and these have been translated into English as 'thorns', 'briers', 'brambles', 'thistles', 'tares', 'nettles', 'cockles', etc. You can never be certain from the context which plant is actually meant (plate 7). That there are so many is due to the desert; these plants flourish in arid areas, just as plants with luxuriant foliage flourish near water. Indeed, much of the flora of the Holy Land is made up of prickly and spiny desert plants. The 'brier' of Isaiah and of Micah 7:4 (*The best of them is as a brier: the most upright is sharper than a thorn hedge'*) is thought to be the Palestinian nightshade or Jericho potato *Solanum incanum* which grows in the Jordan valley and around the Dead Sea.

PLATE II

Spikenard and Saffron, calamus and
Cinnamon ,

SONG of SOL^N. CH IV. part of V^{ER}. XIV.

BULRUSH *Cyperus papyrus (Cyperaceae)*

'*And when she could no longer hide him, she took for him an ark of* bulrushes' (Exodus 2:3).

The 'ark' containing the baby Moses was a papyrus basket; in those days papyrus, or paper sedge (plate 8), grew in profusion along the banks of the Nile. Moses was not alone in sailing, or floating, in a papyrus boat. '*Woe to the land ... that sendeth ambassadors by the sea, even in vessels of* bulrushes *upon the water*' (Isaiah 18:2).

A more famous use of papyrus was in paper-making. Strips of the pith were placed side by side with another layer at right angles; both layers were then pressed together to form a single sheet. The Greeks called the white pith inside the papyrus stalks *byblos* and the books composed of the pith were called *bybla*—hence the word 'Bible'.

The papyrus has smooth three-angled stems and can reach a height of ten to sixteen feet, culminating in a plume of grass-like stalks, each bearing clusters of little brown flower heads. The general effect is often compared with that of a loose household mop.

CAMPHIRE (henna) *Lawsonia inermis*

(*Lythraceae*)

'*My beloved is unto me as a cluster of* camphire *in the vineyards of En-gedi*' (Song of Solomon 1:14).

'*Thy plants are an orchard of pomegranates, with pleasant fruits;* camphire, *with spikenard*' (Song of Solomon 4:13).

The word 'camphire' in the above verses should actually read 'henna'. It is now accepted that the true camphire or camphor (*Cinnamomum camphora*) (plate 9) has nothing to do with the plant eulogized in the Song of Solomon. The camphor tree came from the Far East, in particular Formosa, whence camphor was sent to the mainland for sale, and it reached the western world long after Solomon's day.

The plant of the Song of Solomon is henna (*Lawsonia inermis*), known to the Jews as *kopher* and to the Arabs as *alhenna* and 'Egyptian privet'. It still grows in abundance at Engedi on the Dead Sea, a few miles north of Herod's fortress at Masada, as it did in the days of Solomon. The tropical shrub henna has many small, white, highly scented flowers, hanging in grape-like clusters. Their fragrance had, as we know, a special appeal for Solomon. A nosegay of henna is today a welcome gift to many an eastern lady who,

more likely than not, will take it with her into her bath.

The crushed leaves of the camphire/henna plant provided a powerful dye—light yellow and dark dusky red—which was used to stain the skin and nails of Egyptian mummies. The Children of Israel, in the days of their captivity in Egypt, applied it liberally to their own bodies; the women stained the palms of their hands and the soles of their feet and the men coloured their beards and the manes and tails of their horses. Jewish leaders frowned upon the cosmetic uses of the henna dyes as being pagan in spirit. If a beautiful woman was captured in battle, orders were for her Israelite captors to take her home and give her a thorough scrubbing. '*Then thou shalt bring her home to thine house; and she shall shave her head and pare her nails*' (Deuteronomy 21:12).

CASSIA *Saussurea lappa (Compositae)*

or *Cinnamomum cassia (Lauraceae)*

'*All thy garments smelt of myrrh, and aloes, and* cassia' (Psalms 45:8).

The 'cassia' of the Psalms (plate 2) is not, so the experts say, the same plant which is called 'cassia' in other parts of the Old Testament. In this case the Hebrew word is *ketzioth*; in the others it is *kiddah*. Both words have one thing in common—they derive from a source meaning to cleave or peel off and are applicable to plants such as cassia and cinnamon.

The 'cassia' of the Psalms is the Indian orris (*Saussurea lappa*) from the Himalayas, whose fragrant roots found their way to the Persian Gulf and to Palestine. It is used as a medicine, aphrodisiac and perfume.

'*Take thou also unto thee principal spices ... of* cassia *five hundred shekels*' (Exodus 30:23–24).

'*Dan also and Javan going to and fro occupied in thy fairs: bright iron,* cassia *and calamus were in thy market*' (Ezekiel 27:19).

The 'cassia' of Exodus and Ezekiel is the cassia-bark tree, *Cinnamomum cassia*. This came from Ceylon and the Far East. The precious substance was weighed and valued before being mixed with the other spices of the anointing oil.

PLATE 12

Can the Rush grow up without mire? JOB. Ch VIII. part of Ver. XI.

Who cut up Mallows by the bushes, JOB. Ch XXX. part of Ver. IV.

And Cockle instead of barley. JOB. Ch XXXI. part of Ver. XL.

CHESTNUT (plane tree) *Platanus orientalis*

(Platanaceae)

'*And Jacob took him rods of green poplar and of the hazel and* chestnut tree, *and pilled white strakes in them, and made the white appear which was in the rods*' (Genesis 30:37).

This passage reads with greater botanical accuracy if 'hazel' and 'chestnut' are replaced by 'almond' and 'plane'. It is established that the 'hazel' of Genesis 30:37 is not the true hazel, *Corylus avellana*, but the almond (qv). Similarly the common chestnut, *Castanea sativa*, (plate 10) is not indigenous to Palestine; 'chestnut' in the Bible is the wrong translation of the Hebrew *armôn*, meaning oriental plane tree, *Platanus orientalis*.

The plane is a large tree, sixty or more feet tall, with spreading branches and a smooth bark. *Armôn* is derived from a Hebrew word meaning 'nakedness'. Now, the plane tree periodically sheds its bark, leaving the trunk and branches smooth, white and 'naked'. This is sometimes given as further evidence that the 'chestnut' of the Bible was, in fact, a plane tree. It grows, like poplars and willows, in rich and humid soil beside streams and rivers in Palestine. The common chestnut, on the other hand, prefers dry and hilly situations.

Socrates held forth under a plane tree. It was one of the first exotic trees to be introduced into Europe. The prophet Ezekiel was one of its early admirers: '*The cedars in the garden of God could not hide him: the fir trees were not like his boughs, and the chestnut trees were not like his branches; nor any tree in the garden of God was like unto him in his beauty*' (Ezekiel 31:8).

CINNAMON *Cinnamomum zeylanicum*

(Lauraceae)

'*Spikenard and saffron; calamus and* cinnamon' (Song of Solomon 4:14).

'*And the merchants of the earth shall weep and mourn over her; for no man buyeth their merchandise any more ... all manner vessels of most precious wood ... And* cinnamon, *and odours, and ointments ... The merchants of these things, which were made rich by her, shall stand afar off for the fear of her torment, weeping and wailing*' (Revelation 18:11, 12, 13, 15).

The cinnamon is native to Ceylon, where it is known as *Kornudaganah* (plate 11). It is a member of the laurel family and grows to a height of thirty feet. It is easily recognized by its beautifully veined leaves. The cinnamon of commerce is obtained from the inner bark; quills are cut out of the bark and tied into bundles. The Jews valued it highly as a spice and perfume; it was one of the ingredients of Moses' 'holy oil'.

COCKLE *Agrostemma githago*

'*If my land cry against me, or that the furrows likewise thereof complain; if I have eaten the fruits thereof without money ... let thistles grow instead of wheat, and* cockle *instead of barley*' (Job 31:38-40).

Job is here protesting his integrity and inviting punishment if his behaviour was not all it should have been. There have been several theories as to the identity of Job's 'cockle'—blackberry bushes, poppies, dwarf elder, white aconite, smutted barley, hoary nightshade or noxious weeds in general have all been mentioned. Favoured today is the ordinary corn-cockle, which is common in grain fields. It is an attractive but destructive plant. The flowers are a vivid pink; the stalks are covered with grey down (plate 12); its seeds, if not sifted, will contaminate wheat and barley.

PLATE 13

We remember the fish, which we did eat in

Egypt freely; the Cucumbers, & the Melons,

NUMBERS. CH XI. part of VER V.

CORIANDER *Coriandrum sativum*

(Umbelliferae)

'*And the manna was as* coriander *seed, and the colour thereof as the colour of bdellium*' (Numbers 11:7).

Coriander (plate 9) is only twice mentioned in the Bible and on each occasion in connection with 'manna' which reminded the Israelites, during their wanderings in the Sinai desert, of the appearance of coriander seeds. Both references are in the second and fourth books of Moses, i.e. Exodus and Numbers. '*And the house of Israel called the name thereof Manna: and it was like a* coriander *seed, white; and the taste of it was like wafers made with honey*' (Exodus 16:31). The gift of manna was the Lord's answer to the murmurings of the Children of Israel who had hardly been out of captivity two months before they were reproaching Moses and Aaron for bringing them into the wilderness to die of hunger. The Lord, as ever indulgent, arranged for the face of the land to be covered with 'a small round thing, as small as the hoar frost on the ground'. The Children of Israel 'wist not what it was' and called it 'manna' from the Hebrew *mân hu*, meaning 'What is this?'. This question has never ceased to tease students of the Bible. Let us briefly leave corianders and see how far we can move towards identifying the mysterious 'miraculous' manna, which apparently resembled them.

There are three different kinds of manna mentioned in the Bible. Firstly, there is the 'apocryphal' manna, mentioned in Baruch, which was bought and sold and bartered. '*Behold, we have sent you money to buy you burnt offerings, and sin offerings, and incense, and prepare ye manna, and offer upon the altar of the Lord our God*' (Baruch 1:10). This referred to the resinous or gummy exudations of various desert trees, such as the manna tamarisk (*Tamaria mannifera*) and the spiny camelthorn (*Alhagi camelorum*). It was, to be more precise, the insects feeding on those trees or shrubs which produced this sweet resin. The resin exuded by day hardened at night and could be shaken from the leaves and stems in the early morning. This is still done by Bedouins who sell it to the monks of St Catherine's Monastery on Mount Sinai who, in their turn, use it instead of sugar.

The second type of manna grew up during the night when the ground was moist but 'bred worms and stank' in the morning. This was probably gelatinous algae called *Nostoe* or 'star-jelly'; '*When the sun waxed hot, it melted*' (Exodus 16:21).

The third type of manna was that which 'fell from heaven'. Pundits have identified this as a lichen (*Lecanora*). Sometimes known as 'angels' food' and 'corn of heaven' these *Lecanora* lichens, in periods of heat and drought, detached themselves from their base, curled up into little balls (resembling coriander seeds), were carried along by the wind and then settled or 'rained down' upon some distant territory, such as the Sinai Desert, although they never actually grew there. A final theory is that manna may have been quail-dung. It is, however, unlikely that that would have tasted, then or now, 'like wafers made with honey'!

So much, then, for the various manna theories. We now return to the coriander, the umbelliferous plant with leaves like parsley, known in Hebrew as *gad*. Both its leaves and fruit ('seed' is an incorrect term) are highly aromatic; the former were used in Biblical times, as today, to flavour soups, puddings and wines and the latter was freely sprinkled on bread, cakes and pastry and prized as an aphrodisiac, an attribute dismissed by Victorian writers as 'fanciful'. Gerard in his *Herball* (1597) warns us against the 'venemous qualities' of the coriander fruit.

The Children of Israel likened manna to the coriander 'seed' in shape and to bdellium in colour. We know that the Garden of Eden contained 'bdellium and the onyx stone' (Genesis 2:12). Bdellium is a gum resin obtained from two different species of *Commiphora*, one in Africa and the other in India. We may then take our choice in deciding the location of the Garden of Eden.

PLATE 14

Now learn a parable of the Fig-tree:

When his branch is yet tender, and putteth

forth leaves, ye know that summer is nigh: Mat.ch XXIV.ver XXXII.

CUCUMBER *Cucumis sativus*

(*Cucurbitaceae*)

'*We remember the fish, which we did eat in Egypt freely; the* cucumbers, *and the melons, and the leeks, and the onions, and the garlick*' (Numbers 11:5).

'*And the daughter of Zion is left as a cottage in a vineyard, as a lodge in a garden of* cucumbers, *as a besieged city*' (Isaiah 1:8).

Small wonder that the thoughts of the Israelites, when in the inhospitable desert, should have turned to that cooling fruit which grows in the thick moist mud along the banks of the Nile. They had in mind the common cucumber (in Hebrew *kishuim*) (plate 13). Isaiah's 'garden of cucumbers' is in Hebrew *mikshah*, a cucumber field. Each field contained a raised cottage or a lodge—a crude structure of four poles with walls of woven boughs—from which the watchmen kept a wary eye on potential thieves.

In Egypt and Palestine cucumbers still grow on moist, low-lying land. In summer they are an important part of the people's diet. Every town and village has cucumbers for sale—a good deal smaller than those we grow in our kitchen gardens.

EBONY *Diospyros ebenum* or *D. ebenaster*

(*Ebenaceae*)

'*The men of Dedan were thy merchants; many isles were the merchandise of thine hand: they brought thee for a present horns of ivory and* ebony' (Ezekiel 27:15).

This is the only reference to ebony in the Bible (plate 4). Ezekiel is talking about the prosperity of Tyre, the Venice of the Near East. Precious merchandise came great distances to be traded; Ezekiel gives a dazzling account of the objects to be seen at the market of Tyre.

We think of ebony as something hard and smooth and black and shiny. It comes from the Hebrew *eben*, a stone; the name Ebenezer means 'stone of my help'. Ebony was the heartwood of the *Diospyros ebenum* of Ceylon and Southern India. Phoenician ships brought the ebony up the Persian Gulf where it was transported to Tyre by camel caravan.

The outside wood or sapwood of the ebony tree is soft and white and valueless; it is the interior wood or heartwood which is hard, black, heavy and valuable. A good trunk can yield a heartwood log two feet in diameter and fifteen feet long. Ezekiel mentioned ebony and ivory in the same breath; it was fashionable in those days to inlay ebony with ivory, with striking artistic results.

Ebony is the furniture of the underworld; Pluto's throne was made of ebony and the statues of Egyptian gods and goddesses representing night, darkness and sorrow were carved from this uncompromisingly black wood.

PLATE 15

For the Fitches are not threshed with a threshing instrument,

ISAIAH. Ch XXVIII part of Ver. XXVII.

The kingdom of heaven is like to a grain of Mustard seed, MAT. Ch XIII. part of Ver. XXXI

FIG TREE *Ficus carica (Moraceae)*

'*Now learn a parable of the* fig tree; *when his branch is yet tender, and putteth forth leaves, ye know that summer is nigh*' (Matthew 24:32).

The fig features on several famous occasions in the Bible, in which it has the distinction of being the first plant to be mentioned. '*And the eyes of them both were opened, and they knew that they were naked; and they sewed* fig leaves *together, and made themselves aprons*' (Genesis 3:7). Or, as the Geneva Bible (1560) has it, '*they made themselves breeches*'.

The Hebrew word for the fig tree (plate 14) is *Teenah*, meaning to 'spread out'. Its habits of growth vary; it can crawl like a climber or be a good-sized tree in its own right, when it can be enjoyed for its shade. It has always been usual to have a fig tree in one's garden; it gave shade as well as fruit, and one could sit under it in peace. '*But they shall sit every man under his vine and under his fig tree*' (Micah 4:4).

The fruit of the fig tree is not really a fruit at all; it is a large, fleshy, hollow receptacle which contains the flowers. We know about the fig tree's unreliable fruit-bearing habits, from our own experience and from our Lord's disappointment at finding a fig tree with a great show of leaves but no fruit. It probably reminded him of the hypocrisy of the Pharisees and he 'cursed' it roundly. '*And when he saw a* fig tree *in the way, he came to it, and found nothing thereon, but leaves only, and said unto it, Let no fruit grow on thee henceforward, for ever. And presently the* fig tree *withered away*' (Matthew 21:19).

The fig, the vine and the olive are the most important fruit trees in the Holy Land. Palestine was known as being '*a land of wheat, and barley, and vines, and* fig trees, *and pomegranates*' (Deuteronomy 8:8).

FITCHES *Nigella sativa (Ranunculaceae)*

'*When he hath made plain the face thereof, doth he not cast abroad the* fitches *and scatter the cummin? . . . For the* fitches *are not threshed with a threshing instrument, neither is a cart wheel turned about upon the cummin; but the* fitches *are beaten out with a staff, and the cummin with a rod*' (Isaiah 28:25, 27).

The 'fitches' of Isaiah are not the true fitches or vetches of the genus *Vicia* as drawn in plate 15. The original Hebrew *ketzah* is the black cummin or nutmeg-flower, which grows wild in Palestine and is cultivated for its fragrant aromatic seeds. It belongs to the buttercup family and is closely related to the garden plant love-in-a-mist. This was the plant which Isaiah said must be threshed gently with sticks to avoid damaging the spring seeds. The seeds are still beaten out by the methods advocated by Isaiah.

FLAX *Linum usitatissimum (Linaceae)*

'*A bruised reed shall he not break, and smoking* flax *shall he not quench, till he send forth judgment unto victory*' (Matthew 12:20).

Flax is the world's oldest textile plant (plate 16). The Hebrew word *pishtah* refers to the common flax. Linen is made from the stems of this charming blue-flowered annual, which was an important crop in Egypt and also in Canaan before the arrival of the Israelites. The harlot Rahab brought Joshua's two spies 'up to the roof of the house, and hid them with the stalks of *flax*, which she had laid in order upon the roof' (Joshua 2:6); she later hid them under the flax.

It was the practice to pull up the flax by the roots, tie it into bundles, and soak it in water for several weeks until the outer part decayed. Then by a brushing or combing process the useful fibres were separated from the rest. This was known as 'netting'. The bundles were then opened and the 'netted' stems spread out to dry.

Jewish priests had to wear linen when officiating at sacrifices. '*And the priest shall put on his* linen *garment, and his* linen *breeches*' (Leviticus 6:10) and, much later, our Lord's body was wrapped in a linen shroud. '*And they took the body of Jesus, and wound it in* linen *clothes with the spices, as the manner of Jews is to bury*' (John 19:40).

A bruised Reed shall he not break, and smoking Flax

shall he not quench, till he send forth judgment unto victory.

MAT. Cᴴ. XII . Vᵉʳ XX.

FULLER'S SOAP *Salsola kali*

'*But who may abide the day of his coming? and who shall stand when he appeareth? for he is like a refiner's fire, and like fuller's soap*' (Malachi 3:2).

Soap was made in the Holy Land by burning plants of saltwort, of which the prickly saltwort, *Salsola kali*, was the most common (plate 17). Their ashes, which were rich in potash, were then mixed with olive oil. The Arabic name for saltwort, *kali* or *el kali*, is the source of our word 'alkali'.

The making of soap was, and still is, an important trading activity in Palestine.

GRAPE VINE *Vitis vinifera (Vitidaceae)*

'*I am the true vine, and my father is the husbandman*' (John 15:1).

The vine (plate 18), its fruit and the wine made from it are mentioned constantly in the Bible, from Noah onwards. Noah, indeed, planted a vineyard after the deluge and drank a bit more than was good for him. '*And Noah began to be a husbandman, and he planted a vineyard: and he drank of the wine and was drunken*' (Genesis 9:20–21). The vine, wheat and olive—those essentials of the Holy Land are part of everyone's daily life. '*A land of wheat, and barley, and vines, and fig trees*' (Deuteronomy 8:8). This was the promised land.

The vines of Palestine were famous for their heavy clusters of large juicy grapes. The spies sent by Moses to explore the land of Canaan cut, in the valley of Eschol, near Hebron, a cluster of grapes that was so large '*that they bore it between two upon a staff*' (Numbers 13:23). The Israelites in the wilderness longed for the puny grapes of Egypt—'*And wherefore have ye made us to come up out of Egypt, to bring us into this evil place: it is no place of seed, or of figs, or of vines*' (Numbers 20:9)—unaware of the delicious ones which lay ahead of them. The grape vine is the first cultivated plant to be recorded in the Bible. Its origins are uncertain; botanists say that it came from Armenia, where it still grows with the luxuriant wildness of a tropical creeper, clinging to tall trees and producing abundant fruit without pruning or cultivation.

The vine is honoured before all other plants of the world. 'The fruitful vine' and 'the vine brought out of Egypt' symbolized the Jewish people and our Lord compared himself with the 'true vine' of which His disciples were the branches.

HAZEL *Corylus avellana (Corylaceae)*

'*Jacob took him rods of green poplar, and of the* hazel *and chesnut tree; and pilled white strakes in them, and made the white appear which was in the rods*' (Genesis 30:37).

The common hazel nut is a shrub or low tree; a native of Europe and the Near East, growing to a height of twenty feet or more and often found as undergrowth in woods, especially beneath oaks. There are many varieties of hazel, divided roughly into those cultivated for botanical or ornamental purposes and those cultivated for their fruit.

This particular verse in the Bible, in which the hazel is first mentioned, has caused commentators much trouble. We have said (see Chestnut) that the 'hazel' of Genesis is not the true hazel, *Corylus avellana*, but the almond.

HEATH *Tamarix articulata (Tamaricaceae)*

'*Cursed be the man that trusteth in man . . . for he shall be like the* heath *in the desert, and shall not see when good cometh: but shall inhabit the parched places in the wilderness . . .*' (Jeremiah 17:5–6).

To illustrate Jeremiah's 'heath' McCheane has drawn some typically British heather (*Calluna vulgaris*) (plate 19), which does not occur in Palestine. Jeremiah probably had in mind the tamarisk, a stunted desert bush, or possibly the juniper, which is a common desert plant.

PLATE 17

Under the Nettles they were gathered together, JOB.CH.XXX. part of VER.VII.

For he is like a refiner's Fire and like Fuller's Soap. MAL I. CH III. part of V II.

HEMLOCK *Conium maculatum*

(Umbelliferae)

'They have spoken words, swearing falsely in making a covenant: thus judgement springeth up as hemlock *in the furrows of the field'* (Hosea 10:4).

'Shall horses run upon the rock? will one plow there with oxen? for ye have turned judgement into gall, and the fruit of righteousness into hemlock' (Amos 6:12).

One of hemlock's historical uses was as a death penalty in ancient Greece. Socrates was ordered to kill himself by taking hemlock in 399 BC. Hemlock (plate 20) belongs to the same family as parsley and parsnip, but it is more sinister than those useful and harmless vegetables. It is not a popular plant.

The hemlock is a dark, poisonous biennial (its poisonous properties must not be exaggerated), about five feet tall, with fine, fern-like leaves and tiny white flowers on top of branching stems. It has blood-red blotches on its stem; hence the description *maculatum* (spotted). The seeds contain an oily substance called caria which, if swallowed by human beings, can lead to unfortunate results. When bruised, the hemlock lets out an unpleasant smell.

The Hebrew word for hemlock is *rôsh*. It is also translated as wormwood or gall. All these plants have a bitter taste and are in the Bible, as elsewhere, symbols of bitter calamity and misfortune.

HYSSOP *Origanum maru; Majorana syriaca*

(Labiatae)

'Purge me with hyssop *and I shall be clean: wash me, and I shall be whiter than snow'* (Psalms 51:7).

No botanical term in the Bible has been more argued over than 'hyssop' (plate 20). There appear to be several different plants to which this name has been given.

Many people supposed that the well-known garden herb (*Hyssopus officinalis*) was the biblical plant. They were wrong. Our garden hyssop is indigenous to southern Europe and was not known in the Holy Land or Egypt.

For the 'hyssop' of the Old Testament, these are some of the plants which have been proposed over the years—prickly caper (*Capparis spinosa*); pokeweed (*Phytolacca decandra*); wall rue (*Asplenium ruta-muraria*);

maidenhair spleenwort (*A. trichomanes*) and the Syrian or white marjoram (*Origanum maru*). The latter is now thought to fit most of the scriptural passages which contain the word 'hyssop'. The Hebrew word *ezob* sounds like the Greek *hyssopus*, which was the translation used by the writer of the Septuagint (those seventy 'inspired' men) in the fourth century, whom we have to thank for this confusion.

The psalmist's prayer, *'Purge me with* hyssop' (Psalms 51:7), unless it is to be interpreted literally as a laxative, is an allusion to the purificatory use of the plant. The same words are, or were, used in Catholic churches (*Asperges me, Domine, hyssopo, et mundabor,* 'Thou shalt sprinkle me with hyssop, O Lord, and I shall be cleansed'). Furthermore, the brush used for sprinkling holy water is called a 'hyssop'.

Marjorams are members of the mint family (*Labiatae*), along with the Judaean sage, which some say inspired the seven-branched 'candlestick'. They are fragrant, wiry plants, up to three feet in height, but much less when growing, as they often do, in rocky crevices or poor soil. They have hairy branches and leaves and white flowers. Thanks to their hairy stems, they hold water very well; this is why they were used as sprinklers in religious ceremonies and Jewish sacrificial rites. Moses directed that the 'hyssop' be used to sprinkle the doorposts of the Israelites in Egypt with the blood of the paschal lamb so that the angel of death would pass by that house (Exodus 12:22). It was also used for cleansing lepers (Leviticus 14:4).

Solomon's remarkable activities embraced botanical and zoological knowledge. *'And he spake of trees, from the cedar tree that is in Lebanon even unto the* hyssop *that springeth out of the wall: he spake also of beasts, and of fowl, and of creeping things, and of fishes'* (I Kings 4:33). Here the 'hyssop' is used to show that even the most modest plant was not too insignificant to escape the great man's botanical attention.

The 'hyssop' of the Crucifixion passages has occasioned many botanical controversies, although none has as yet sparked off a religious war. *'Now there was set a vessel full of vinegar: and they filled a spunge with vinegar, and put it upon* hyssop, *and put it to his mouth'* (John 19:29). Matthew and Mark say the sponge was put on a 'reed'. The 'hyssop' or 'reed' on which the sponge of vinegar was placed could not have been marjoram, which was much too small, but must have been a dhura cane or stalk (*Sorghum bicolor*), a tall cereal, known in Palestine as 'Jerusalem corn'. It is a tall plant with strong stems, over six feet in height. The grains from its wide, ribbon-like leaves are used for making coarse beads.

PLATE 18

I am the true Vine, and my Father is the husbandman.

JOHN. Ch XV. ver. I.

JUNIPER *Retama raetam (Leguminosae)*

'*Sharp arrows of the mighty, with coals of* juniper' (Psalms 120:4).

'*But he himself went a day's journey into the wilderness, and came and sat down under a* juniper *tree*' (I Kings 19:4).

The Hebrew word *rotem* or *rothem* is wrongly translated as 'juniper' (plate 21). In other versions it is translated as 'broom'. It is a shrubby plant with pink-and-white blossoms and grows around the Dead Sea, in the Jordan valley and in Sinai, where it is sometimes the only plant affording any shade. Elijah, when fleeing from Jezebel, rested under the shade of a *rotem* or broom, as have many later travellers in the desert (I Kings 19:4). The expression 'coals of juniper' is a reference to the use of the plant as charcoal. Whether as charcoal or as wood, it has a reputation for burning very well.

According to Job people, if desperate, fed on the roots. He found it particularly hard to bear that he was even despised by those 'who cut up mallows by the bushes, and *juniper* roots for their meat' (Job 30:4).

LENTIL *Lens esculenta (Leguminosae)*

'*And Jacob sod pottage: and Esau came from the field, and he was faint: And Esau said to Jacob, Feed me, I pray thee, with that same red pottage; for I am faint: therefore was his name called Edom. And Jacob said, Sell me this day thy birthright. And Esau said, Behold, I am at the point to die; and what profit shall this birthright do to me? And Jacob said, Swear to me this day; and he sware unto him: and he sold his birthright unto Jacob. Then Jacob gave Esau bread and pottage of* lentils; *and he did eat and drink, and rose up, and went his way: thus Esau despised his birthright*' (Genesis 25:29–34).

Here we read how Jacob tricked his brother by offering red lentil stew. Lentils (plate 20), of the pea and bean family, are one of the favourite Old Testament vegetables.

The Hebrew word for lentil is *adashim*, a plural name from the verb *adash* 'to tend a flock', meaning that lentils were food for peasants and herdsmen.

The lentil plant is a small vetch-like annual. Lentils, which are borne in pea-like pods, are flattened and convex on both sides. They have given their name to the lens in a magnifying glass. Lentils are said to supply the most nutritious food of all vegetables, being able to restore tissues in bone, muscle, nerve and brain. They have grown in the Holy Land since time immemorial. As food, they are mixed with flour and baked into bread or made into porridge, or pottage. Esau's pottage was not really 'red', but rather a yellow-brown, which Palestinians preferred to call red.

For he shall be like the heath in the desert, and shall not see when good cometh. JERH. CH XVII, part of VER. VI.

LILIES OF THE FIELD

Anemone coronaria (Ranunculaceae)

'*And why take ye thought for raiment? Consider the* lilies *of the field, how they grow; they toil not, neither do they spin. And yet I say unto you, that even Solomon in all his glory was not arrayed like one of these*' (Matthew 6:28–29).

The poppy anemone (*Anemone coronaria*) is almost certainly the lily of the field of these verses. Alas, our talented artist has drawn a beautiful English lily (plate 22), but it is not a Bible plant. He is not, it is true, the first artist to illustrate this beautiful parable with English garden lilies. He is in good company, including Leonardo da Vinci and many Victorian artists.

Certain alternatives to the poppy anemone have been proposed. One is the white-rayed chamomile, *Anthemis palaestina* of the *Compositae* family. The charm of this daisy-like plant only became obvious at the time of hay-gathering which might have illustrated our Lord's point more effectively than the showy poppy anemone. Another is the glorious scarlet poppy, *Papaver* species of the *Papaveraceae* family. The poppy anemone, Palestine anemone or windflower, to give some different names for *Anemone coronaria*, covers the ground with brilliant blossom in early spring. It is the most conspicuous of all spring flowers. Walking at this season in the Holy Land, among the olives and through fields of thistles and wild grass, I was often hit by an unexpected flash of red—it was the anemone, the 'lily of the field' of our Lord's discourse.

LILY OF THE VALLEY

Hyacinthus orientalis (common hyacinth);
Lilium candidum (Madonna lily)

'*I am the rose of Sharon and the* lily *of the valley. As the* lily *among thorns, so is my love among the daughters*' (Song of Solomon 2:1–2).

Unfortunately, our gifted artist knew little about the botany of the Holy Land. He has drawn for us a typically English lily-of-the-valley (*Convallaria majalis*) (plate 23) which was unknown in Palestine. He may be forgiven for being misled by Solomon's 'lily of the valleys', whose identity continues to baffle scholars. Many authors have thought it to be the same plant as the 'lily of the fields' (*Anemone coronaria*) and others have identified it as a violet, jasmine or buttercup.

It is now thought likely that Solomon had in mind the garden hyacinth for the 'lily' in the above verses— plants which grew in the grassy fields—and the Madonna lily for those which grew in woods or were cultivated in well shaded gardens. '*My beloved is gone down into his garden, to the beds of spices, to feed in the gardens, and to gather* lilies. *I am my beloved's, and my beloved is mine: he feedeth among the* lilies. *Thou art beautiful, O my love, as Tirzah, comely as Jerusalem ...*' (Song of Solomon 6:2–4).

The discovery earlier this century of a genuine wild plant of *Lilium candidum* in a shady spot in northern Palestine gave welcome support to the theory that Solomon was familiar with the Madonna lily. Until then there had been no record of its having existed in Palestine. Christians have always wished passionately to believe that the white Madonna lily, which the archangel Gabriel invariably carries in pictures of the Annunciation, was a legitimate Bible plant, but they got no comfort from botanists on this score. Now, however, botanical faith is botanical fact and we may think of Solomon's 'lilies' as the deep blue fragrant hyacinths which cover the hills of Galilee in the spring or as the majestic Madonna lily, symbol of innocence, virginity and purity, fit for the garden of a rich and powerful king.

PLATE 20

Thus judgment springeth up as Hemlock, HOSEA.Cʰ X part of.Vᵉʳ IV.

Purge me with Hyssop, and I shall be clean: Psm. LI part.of Vᵉʳ VII.

Then Jacob gave Esau bread and pottage of Lentiles. GᴱNˢCʰXXVᵥₑᵣVᵈ
XXXIV

MALLOWS *Atriplex halimus*

'*But now they that are younger than I have me in derision, whose fathers I would have disdained to have set with the dogs of my flock ... who cut up* mallows *by the bushes, and juniper roots for their meat*' (Job 30:1, 4).

Job is casting his mind back to the days when his present tormentors were unworthy of his notice. He remembers their lowly pursuits such as gathering mallows, in this instance a species of saltwort known as 'sea purblane', a bushy shrub related to the spinach. It grows on the shores of the Mediterranean and about the Dead Sea. The Hebrew word is *malluach*, implying saltiness of taste or location. Job lived in the 'land of Uz', north-east of the Gulf of Aqaba, where many such 'mallows' are to be found. They are not, unfortunately, the true mallows of the genus *Malva* shown in the illustration (plate 12), which do not occur in the Holy Land.

MANDRAKE *Mandragora officinarum*

(Solonaceae)

'*And Reuben went in the days of the wheat harvest, and found* mandrakes *in the field, and brought them unto his mother Leah. Then Rachel said to Leah, Give me, I pray thee, of thy son's* mandrakes' (Genesis 30:14).

The mandrake (plate 21), or love-apple (in Hebrew *dudaim*) has been the subject of stranger stories than any other plant. This relatively harmless member of the potato family and relation of the tomato has struck superstitious terror into people throughout the ages because its forked, rugged root resembles the lower half of the human body. It was said to scream if touched. The only safe way to uproot a mandrake, according to Josephus, was to tie a dog to the plant; in running after its master, the dog would pull the mandrake out of the ground and then die of convul-

sions. The master then had the root which protected him against evil spirits.

The mandrake's resemblance to the lower, 'reproductive', portions of the human body won for it a reputation as an aphrodisiac. It excited voluptuousness and induced fertility. Hence the childless Rachel's anxiety to secure some of her nephew's mandrakes (Genesis 30:14). Whether Jacob and Rachel jointly nibbled at the love plant is not clear—we must assume they ate the red rather sickly tasting 'love-apple' and not the slightly poisonous root—but it had the desired result: God 'opened her womb' and the result was Joseph.

The mandrake flowers early in the year and its fruits are like small yellow eggs on the ground, nesting in large, wrinkled, dark-green leaves. The yellow, purple-veined flowers are like those of the potato. It is a native of the eastern Mediterranean.

MELON *Citrullus vulgaris* (water-melon);

Cucumis melo (musk-melon)

'*We remember the fish, which we did eat in Egypt freely; the cucumbers, and the* melons ... *but now our soul is dried away: there is nothing at all, beside this manna, before our eyes* (Numbers 11:5–6).

Only once does the Bible mention the fruit after which the Israelites thirsted in the desert. Opinion is divided as to whether they longed for the water-melon or the musk-melon, which is now also called the canteloupe (plate 13). Probably both. The musk-melon came originally from India and has been cultivated in Egypt for thousands of years. It was introduced to England in the sixteenth century.

The water-melon is a native of central Africa and has also been grown in Egypt since time immemorial. You see them now on the plain between Haifa and Jaffa, the vines supported by sticks to prevent the plants crashing down under the weight of melons which may weigh up to thirty pounds.

PLATE 21

Sharp arrows of the mighty, with coals of Juniper. PSALM.CXX. VER. IV.

Then Rachel said to Leah, give me, I pray thee of thy sons
Mandrakes. GENS. CH.XXX. part of VER. XIV.

MINT *Mentha longifolia (Labiatae)*

'*But woe unto you, Pharisees! for ye tithe* mint *and rue and all manner of herbs, and pass over judgment and the love of God*' (Luke 11:42).

This herb is only twice mentioned in the Bible—in the above passage and in a corresponding one in Matthew 23:23. Various species of the mint family (*Labiatae*) were used for flavouring in New Testament times. The illustration (plate 24) shows garden mint, a cultivated form of the wild horsemint, *Mentha longifolia*, which is common in the ditches and banks of Palestine. Other Palestinian mints are peppermint and pennyroyal. According to Pliny the garden mint could be used in forty-one remedies; it was used by Jews, Greeks and Romans as a flavouring in many dishes. In a Roman cookery book written in the early years AD, it is mentioned on almost every page. The Jews scattered mint on the floors of their synagogues, so that the perfume oozed out at each step. Indeed, all members of the mint family are highly scented: thyme, basil, marjoram, sage, lavender, patchouli, etc.

MULBERRY *Morus nigra (Moraceae)*

'*Therefore David inquired again of God; and God said unto him, Go not up after them; turn away from them, and come upon them over against the* mulberry *trees. And it shall be, when thou shalt hear a sound of going in the tops of the* mulberry *trees, that then thou shalt go out to battle: for God is gone forth before thee to smite the host of Philistines*' (I Chronicles 14:14–15).

Unfortunately, the black mulberry (*Morus nigra*) shown in plate 25 has nothing to do with the 'mulberry trees' of these verses from I Chronicles. This is one of many examples of the botanical ignorance of the authors of the King James's Version. They called aspens, or poplars, 'mulberries' and they called mulberries 'sycamines'.

The 'mulberry' of the picture is indeed the 'sycamine' of Luke (17:6). The apostle asked how they could strengthen their faith. '*And the Lord said, If ye have faith as a grain of mustard seed, ye might say unto this* sycamine *tree, Be thou plucked up by the root, and be thou planted in the sea; and it should obey you.*' It is emphatically not, as some have thought, the 'sycomore' which Zacchaeus scrambled up in Luke 19:4 to get a good view of our Lord. This was the sycomore-fig or mulberry-fig (*Ficus sycomorus*), a robust evergreen frequently seen along roadsides in the Holy Land.

Luke's 'sycamine', the black mulberry, (in Hebrew *shikmah*) is cultivated everywhere in the Holy Land for its large, delicious blackberry-like fruit. The juice, being blood-red, was used in Antioch to goad the elephants into action. '*And to the end they might provoke the elephants to fight, they shewed them the blood of grapes and mulberries*' (I Maccabees 6:34).

The white mulberry (*Morus alba*) comes from China and only reached the Mediterranean in the Middle Ages. It soon supplanted the black mulberry as food for silkworms. The cultivation of mulberries for raising silkworms is, therefore, a relatively recent matter. The first mention of silk, as opposed to linen, in the Bible occurs in Ezekiel (16:10, 13), nearly five hundred years after Solomon. '. . . and I covered thee with silk . . . and thy raiment was of fine linen, and silk, and broidered work.' It is difficult to believe that Solomon, who luxuriated in all that was fine and opulent, never knew the joys of caressing silk. But there it is.

The 'mulberry trees', in whose tops the sound of a 'going' was heard, are aspens or trembling poplars (*Populus euphratica*), called in Hebrew *becaim*. The rustling of their leaves was, as we have read, the sign for David's troops to attack the Philistines. Hence the expression 'trembling poplar'. The trembling of the leaf in the slightest breeze is botanically explained by the flattening of the petioles or leaf-stalks. The leaves of the real mulberry (*Morus nigra*) are soft-textured and borne on a firm round petiole and cannot therefore make the 'sound of going' when stirred by the breeze. These trees are common in the Jordan valley and indeed throughout the country.

PLATE 22

Consider the Lilies of the Field, how they grow:

MAT.Ch.VI. part of Ver XXVIII

MUSTARD *Brassica nigra (Cruciferae)*

'*The kingdom of heaven is like to a grain of* mustard seed, *which a man took, and sowed in his field: which indeed is the least of all seeds: but when it is grown, it is the greatest among herbs, and becometh a tree, so that the birds of the air come and lodge in the branches thereof*' (Matthew 13:31–32).

The mustard seed in this exquisite two-verse parable is the plant known as black mustard, *Brassica nigra* (plate 15). Galilee in the spring is splashed with vivid yellow mustard groves; travellers have reported riding through such groves when the plants towered over horse and rider and in which the birds actually *did* build their nests. The seeds produced oil as well as mustard. The only occasions when mustard seed are mentioned are when our Lord compared it to the Kingdom of Heaven and to faith. '*If ye have faith as of a grain of* mustard seed, *ye shall say unto this mountain, remove hence to yonder place; and it shall remove; and nothing shall be impossible unto you*' (Matthew 17:20).

MYRRH *Commiphora myrrha (Burseraceae)*

'*All thy garments smell of* myrrh, *and aloes and cassia, out of ivory palaces, whereby they have made thee glad*' (Psalms 45:8).

The substance myrrh (in Hebrew *mor*) is a fragrant gum which is exuded from trees in Arabia, Abyssinia and Somaliland. The myrrh tree (plate 2) is a low thorny shrub which grows on rocky places. Although the gum exudes naturally from the stems and branches, it will flow more freely if incisions are made in the wood. The spontaneously exuding liquid was, according to Pliny, the most superior kind of myrrh. It comes out of the tree as a soft, clear, sticky, yellowish-brown resin; at first rather oily, it solidifies after falling to the ground. In the East it is highly thought of as a perfume, medicine and embalming ingredient. Some say that the myrrh of the early books of the Bible was probably ladanum from 'rock roses' (*Cistus laurifolius*).

The ladanum split all over the plant and was then collected from the beards of goats who had been browsing on the foliage. A quaint piece of information!

The first mention of myrrh in the Bible was in Exodus when the Lord instructed Moses to prepare a holy anointing oil, of which myrrh was an ingredient together with cinnamon and cassia (Exodus 30:23). Solomon revelled in its use. '*I rose up to open to my beloved; and my hands dropped with* myrrh, *and my fingers with sweet smelling* myrrh ... *His cheeks are as a bed of spices, as sweet flowers: his lips like lilies, dropping sweet smelling* myrrh' (Song of Solomon 5:5, 13).

In the New Testament myrrh features on some famous occasions. It was among the gifts brought by the wise men to the infant Jesus (Matthew 2:11); on the Cross '*they gave him to drink wine mingled with* myrrh: *but he received it not*' (Mark 15:23); finally, Nicodemus took one hundred pounds weight of myrrh mixed with powdered aloe leaves, to embalm our Lord's body in the garden tomb after the Crucifixion.

MYRTLE *Myrtus communis (Myrtaceae)*

'*Instead of the thorn shall come up the fir tree, and instead of the brier shall come up the* myrtle *tree*' (Isaiah 55:13).

The myrtle (plate 7) is common in Galilee and Samaria. It was esteemed by the Jews for its beautiful snow-white flowers, dark green foliage and pleasant scent. Its buds and berries were used as spices and distilled water was prepared from its flowers. Isaiah understandably found it a desirable alternative to the brier, or desert thorn. The Jews have for centuries used its evergreen branches for the construction of booths at the Feast of Tabernacles. '*Go forth unto the mount, and fetch olive branches, and pine branches, and* myrtle *branches, and palm branches, and branches of thick trees, to make booths, as it is written*' (Nehemiah 8:15). Zechariah in his vision speaks of '*the angel of the Lord that stood among the* myrtle *trees*' (Zechariah 1:11), as if they were well known.

PLATE 23

I am the Rose of Sharon and the Lily of the valleys.

NETTLE *Urtica urens (Urticaceae)*

'*Among the bushes they brayed; under the* nettles *they were gathered together*' (Job 30:37).

'*And thorns shall come up in her palaces,* nettles *and brambles in the fortresses thereof: and it shall be an habitation of dragons, and a court for owls*' (Isaiah 34:13).

The Hebrew *charul* has been translated in different versions of the Bible as 'nettles', 'scrub', 'briers', 'thorns' and 'weeds'. It is used in connection with desolate places. It has been suggested that Job's 'nettles' (plate 17) are not the true nettle, *Urtica urens*, because people would be unlikely to 'gather together' among such virulently stinging plants. Commentators of this school of thought favour the acanthus. On the other hand, the people among the nettles are meant to be having a miserable time and the more they are stung the better.

OLIVE *Olea europaeae (Oleaceae)*

'*And the dove came to him in the morning; and, lo, in her mouth was an* olive *leaf pluckt off: so Noah knew that the waters were abated from the earth*' (Genesis 8:11).

This is the first of innumerable mentions of the olive and its products in the Bible. It was a sign that the Lord's anger, in the form of the waters, had abated and that he now felt more conciliatory towards what remained of the human race. Thus the olive branch became a symbol of peace. Few trees in the world give greater visual pleasure than the olive; whether on hillside terraces in the Holy Land or in Tuscany, their knobbly trunks and the shimmering grey-green beauty of their leaves give an impression of beauty and timelessness. '*His beauty shall be as the* olive *tree*' (Hosea 14:6).

The olive was an essential tree in the Holy Land, closely associated with the people's daily life. One tree would supply a whole family with fats. Like the vine, that other plant so important in household life, the olive acquired its own symbolism. It was the oil for anointing kings. '*Then Samuel took a vial of oil, and poured it upon his* [Saul's] *head*' (I Samuel 10:1).

The olive tree provided a setting for those later sacred and glorious events in the world's history. The Mount of Olives, outside Jerusalem, was named in Zechariah 14:4 as the spot on which the Saviour's feet would stand. It was there that our Lord retired alone or with His disciples and it was there that the disciples witnessed His ascension into Heaven (Acts 1:12). It is said that some of the olive trees on the Mount of Olives and in Gethsemane have been there since the

days of our Lord. This is not impossible, since the tree lives to a great age.

There are several varieties of olive in the Holy Land. The trees are twenty to thirty feet high with gnarled trunks and smooth ash-coloured barks. All have leathery green leaves and small, whitish flowers. Almost every Palestinian village has its olive grove or olive 'garden'.

PALM TREE *Pheonix dactylifera*

'*The righteous shall flourish like a* palm tree*: he shall grow like a cedar in Lebanon*' (Psalms 92:12).

Palms (plate 26) used to be as plentiful in Palestine as they still are in Egypt; there was a seven-mile-long grove of palms near Jericho, the 'city of palms', in the days of Josephus in the first century AD; the Jordan valley from the Sea of Galilee to the Dead Sea was covered with date palms. They spread over vast areas of the Holy Land, but drought and neglect over the years has wrought such havoc that they are now rarely seen. The palm excites in us westerners a feeling of tropical excitement—the lovely palm in the desert where the weary traveller dismounts from his camel to sit in its shade; the palm on the sea front, its fronds gently ruffled by the warm breezes.

For the Jews the palm had both practical usefulness and symbolic significance. Its Hebrew name is *tamar*. It must be the most extraordinary of all trees. For the Jews it symbolized grace and elegance; girls were named Tamar after it. A single upright trunk may rise up to one hundred feet; it has no branches but its top is crowned by fan-shaped leaves, beneath which the dates grow in clusters. It is an exceptionally valuable plant, providing starch, sugar, oil, wax, and fruit; mats are woven from its leaves; paper and thread are made from its fibres; and liquor is extracted from its sap. When growing in the desert, it indicates the presence of water. The Israelites, on the journey from Egypt, '*came to Elim, where were twelve wells of water, and threescore and ten* palm *trees: and they encamped there by the waters*' (Exodus 15:27). Its large, feathery leaves or 'branches' were used as emblems of victory or triumph; when our Lord entered Jerusalem the people '*took branches of* palm *trees, and went forth to meet him*' (John 12:13). In the heavenly Jerusalem, the great multitude which stood before the Lamb was '*clothed with white robes, and* palms *in their hands*' (Revelation 7:9).

𝕭ut woe unto you, Pharisees! For ye tithe 𝕸int and 𝕽ue and all manner of herbs. LUKE. Chᵃ XI, part of Vᵉʳ XLII.

POMEGRANATE *Punica granatum (Punicaceae)*

'*A land of wheat, and barley, and vines, and fig trees, and* pomegranates' (Deuteronomy 8:8).

'*Thy plants are an orchard of* pomegranates, *with pleasant fruits, camphire with spikenard*' (Song of Solomon 4:13).

The Old Testament abounds in references to the pomegranate (in Hebrew *rimmon*). Moses, in the above verse from Deuteronomy, mentions it as one of the desirable features of the Promised Land and Solomon, that poetic monarch, adorned his Song of Songs with allusions to both the fruit and the flowers of that beautiful plant. '*Thy temples are like a piece of a* pomegranate *within thy locks*' (4:3). '*Let us see if the vine flourish, whether the tender grape appear, and the* pomegranates *bud forth; there will I give thee my loves*' (7:12). The pomegranate (plate 27) is not native to Palestine, although it is quite common there, particularly around Abraham's town of Hebron. It could be traced to Afghanistan via Syria and Persia. We know that it must have grown in Egypt during the Captivity, since the Israelites lamented violently its absence, and that of some other good things, when in the wilderness of Zin. '*And wherefore have ye made us to come up out of Egypt, to bring us into this evil place? It is no place of seed, or of figs, or of vines, or of* pomegranates; *neither is there any water to drink*' (Numbers 20:5).

The word pomegranate comes from *pomum granatum*, or 'grained apple' of the Romans. This name refers to the many red seeds embedded in the juicy pulp visible through the thin rind of its red-coloured fruit, the size of an orange. The tree itself is small and bush-like; the leaves are deep green and the flowers are scarlet. The pulp of the pomegranate has been used since the days of Solomon for making cooling drinks or sherbets. '*I would cause thee to drink of spiced wine of the juice of my* pomegranates' (Song of Solomon 8:2). The rind of the fruit has been used for the dissimilar purposes of curing tape-worms and tanning leather. The Moors introduced into Spain the method of tanning leather with pomegranate rinds and this was one reason for the superiority of Morocco leather, especially for binding books.

The pomegranate came to be regarded as a sacred plant early in Man's history and its fruits and flowers were used as models for decorating both the pillars of Solomon's temple and the hem of the high priest's robes. '*And four hundred* pomegranates *for the two networks, even two rows of* pomegranates *for one network, to cover the two bowls of the chapiters that were upon the pillars*' (I Kings 7:42). '*And they made upon the hems of the robes* pomegranates *of blue, and purple, and scarlet, and twined linen*' (Exodus 39:24).

The pomegranate has always had a part to play in pagan mythologies and old wives' tales. Its seeds became symbols of fecundity or the opposite. The Greeks and Romans held that the bleakness of the winter months was caused by the seeds of the pomegranate germinating in the nether world. In Turkey it is the custom for a bride to throw a ripe pomegranate to the ground and the number of seeds that spill out indicate the number of children she will have.

PLATE 25

Turn away from them, and come upon them over against the Mulberry trees. I. Chrons. Ch. XIV part of Ver. XIV

POPLAR *Populus alba (Salicareae)*

'*And Jacob took him rods of green* poplar ...' (Genesis 30:37).

Jacob peeled off the bark of white poplar (plate 10), in addition to plane and almond, so that the streaked twigs would increase the number of pied animals in his herds. The strange, not very creditable, story of Jacob and the rods is hard to visualize, particularly as told in the rather archaic language of the Authorized Version. It shows that people nearly four thousand years ago believed in the effect of prenatal influences on pregnant females. Jacob 'pilled white strakes', i.e. peeled white stripes in the fresh boughs of poplar, almond and plane, and placed them in the sheep's drinking troughs; as they bred where they drank, their offspring were subsequently 'ringstraked, speckled, and spotted'.

The white poplar is one of several species growing in the hills and in the wet places of Palestine, where it grows to between thirty and sixty feet high. The flowers, in the form of catkins, appear before the leaves and the buds are covered with a resinous varnish; when burnt they give out a balsamic odour.

REED *Arundo donax (Gramineae)*

'*A bruised* reed *shall he not break* ...' (Matthew 12:20).

Matthew is here reminding us of Isaiah's prophecy of the coming of the Lord (Isaiah 42:3). Better known is our Lord's question to the multitudes, '*What went ye out into the wilderness to see? A* reed *shaken with the wind?*' (Matthew 11:7).

The reed depicted in plate 16 is the true reed or giant reed or 'bulrush', *Arundo donax*. This gigantic grass forms dense thickets throughout Palestine and the Sinai peninsula; it grows up to eighteen feet and its lofty stems can bend to the ground before a high wind.

ROSE (narcissus) *Narcissus tazetta*

(Amaryllidaceae)

'*The wilderness and the solitary place shall be glad for them; and the desert shall rejoice, and blossom as the* rose. *It shall blossom abundantly, and rejoice even with joy and singing: the glory of Lebanon shall be given unto it, the excellency of Carmel and Sharon, they shall see the glory of the Lord, and the excellency of our God*' (Isaiah 35:1–2).

One thing is clear after centuries of argument about the identity of the 'rose' in the Bible—it could have been one of several plants, but never a rose, as we understand the word, i.e. 'Rose' is not the genus *Rosa* (plate 28). Isaiah's 'rose' is a bulbous plant and therefore no rose. The Hebrew word for it is *Habazzeleth*, a compound of two words meaning 'acrid bulb'. The early English translators of the Bible were not botanically trained and mistook the hips of the rose for bulbs.

Isaiah's 'rose' has been narrowed down to a crocus, tulip or narcissus. The accepted view is that it is the last, the white or polyanthus narcissus (*Narcissus tazetta*). The white narcissus is an abundant Palestinian plant which grows in Caesarea and the uplands of central Palestine and at Jerusalem or Jericho, where the flowers are a dazzling golden yellow, rather than white or cream-coloured, as in cooler climates. January is its flowering month.

We all know about the Narcissus (Narkissos) of Greek mythology—how he failed to return the love of the nymph Echo, the daughter of Earth and Air, how she pined away leaving nothing but her voice, and how the handsome Narcissus was drowned through admiring his own reflection in the water. A white narcissus sprang up at the spot where his body floated to the shore.

Isaiah's rose has been perversely translated in the New English Bible as 'asphodel', a member of the lily family. This need not shake our resolve to stick steadfastly to the polyanthus narcissus.

PLATE 26

And lo in her mouth was an Olive leaf plucked off: GEN. Cʰ. VIII part of Vᵉʳ XI.

The righteous shall Flourish like a Palm-tree: PSALM. XCII part of Vᵉʳ XII.

ROSE OF SHARON *Tulipa montana,*

T. sharonensis (Liliaceae)

'I am the rose of Sharon, and the lily of the valleys' (Song of Solomon 2:1).

Solomon's 'rose of Sharon' (plate 23) is no more a member of the genus *Rosa* than is Isaiah's 'rose'. It is, in all probability, the mountain tulip, which grows not only in the hills but on the Sharon coastal plain between Carmel and Jaffa. It is a handsome plant, ten inches high, with silver grey-green leaves and glowing red flowers, rather pale outside but crimson within.

The 'roses' of the apocryphal Ecclesiasticus—'And as the flower of roses is the spring of the year . . .' (50:8)—are also thought to be mountain tulips.

RUE *Ruta graveolens (Rutaceae)*

'But woe unto you, Pharisees! for ye tithe mint and rue *and all manner of herbs'* (Luke 11:42).

In the corresponding passage of Matthew 23:23, our Lord joined anise and cummin to those spices which were carefully tithed by the Scribes and Pharisees, who neglected justice and the love of God. The common rue, *Ruta graveolens* (*graveolens* means 'strong smelling'), is very rankly scented—some people hate the smell—and has grey-green leaves throughout the year and yellow flowers in summer (plate 24). As a wild plant, the rue had been free of tithe, but by our Lord's day it had begun to be cultivated and was therefore subject to tithe.

Rue was a plant highly prized by the ancients. Its strong smell gave it perhaps an undeserved reputation for efficacy in medicine and in other respects. By carrying a bundle of rue, you could recognize a witch at a glance; it drove away plagues and girls who nibbled at it found themselves better able to resist seduction. It healed the stings of bees and scorpions and the bites of serpents—so much so that, before a weasel attacked a snake, it took the precaution, according to Pliny, of eating some rue. Because the word 'rue' has two meanings, the one referring to the plant, the other meaning 'repentance', the plant acquired the name 'herb of grace' in the sixteenth century.

RUSH *Juncus effusus (Juncaceae)*

'Can the rush *grow up without mire?'* (Job 8:11).

The soft or bog rush (plate 12) is found in most wet places in Palestine; there are many varieties. The common rush (i.e. soft or bog rush) is over four feet high; its whip-like leaves have been used for centuries to make baskets.

SAFFRON *Crocus sativus (Iridaceae)*

'Spikenard and saffron, *calamus and cinnamon'* (Song of Solomon 4:14).

This is the only mention of saffron (plate 11) in the Bible. The word comes from the Arabic *zafran* meaning 'yellow'. Saffron is the yellow, or rather deep-orange substance, contained in the stigmas which are collected as soon as the flower opens. Four thousand stigmas are needed to make an ounce of saffron; this gives us an idea of the hideous devastation wrought in its habitats in Greece and other parts of Asia Minor, when the mauve petals open in the early autumn.

At the time of Solomon, saffron may have been a drug imported into Palestine. Its main uses, however, then and now, were as a yellow dye and for colouring curries and stews; the stigmas are dried in the sun, packed tightly together and made into cake saffron.

It is unlikely that saffron has been prepared from the stigmas of any other variety of crocus.

Calamus, another of the plants mentioned in the Song of Solomon 4:14 but not illustrated here, is the 'sweet flag' *Acorus calamus (Araceae)*, a member of the arum family, a soft-stemmed aquatic plant which grows in muddy spots and marshes. It is highly aromatic, with flat iris-like leaves.

Thy plants are an orchard of Pomegranates

with pleasant Fruits; SOLOMONS SONG. Ch IV part of Ver XIII.

SPIKENARD *Nardostachys jatamansi*

(Valerianaceae)

'*Thy plants are an orchard of pomegranates, with pleasant fruits; camphire with* spikenard, spikenard *and saffron . . .* (Song of Solomon 4:13–14).

'*And being in Bethany in the house of Simon the leper, as he sat at meat, there came a woman having an alabaster box of ointment of* spikenard *very precious . . .*' (Mark 14:3).

'*Then took Mary a pound of ointment of* spikenard, *very costly, and anointed the feet of Jesus, and wiped his feet with her hair: and the house was filled with the odour of the ointment*' (John 12:3).

The 'spikenard' (plate 11) of these references comes from the stem of the perennial Himalayan valerian (in Hebrew *nard*), which grows in the mountain ranges of Nepal and Bhutan. The roots and stems are dried for making the perfume before the leaves unfold. In view of the long distances it had to travel, spikenard, or spike-nard, was very precious. It was carried by camels in alabaster boxes which preserved the scent. When a host received distinguished guests, he anointed them with spikenard. The suffix *stachys*, meaning in Greek an ear of wheat, refers to the plant's spike-like woolly stems.

TARES *Lolium temulentem (Gramineae)*

'*. . . The kingdom of heaven is likened unto a man which sowed good seed in his field: But while men slept, his enemy came and sowed* tares *among the wheat, and went his way. But when the blade was sprung up, and brought forth fruit, then appeared the* tares *also. So the servants of the householder came and said unto him, Sir, didst not thou sow good seed in the field? from whence then hath it* tares? *He said unto them, An enemy hath done this. The servants said unto him, Wilt thou that we go and gather them up? But he said, Nay; lest while ye gather up the* tares, *ye root up also the wheat with them. Let both grow together until the harvest: and in the time of harvest I will say to the reapers, Gather ye together first the* tares, *and bind them in bundles to burn them: but gather the wheat into my barn*' (Matthew 13:24–30).

The weeds which grew among the wheat in our Lord's 'parable of the tares' were darnel grass (*Lolium temulentum*), also known as bearded darnel and rye grass, which is almost indistinguishable from wheat or rye in its early stages, although its seeds are much smaller (plate 29). If darnel seeds are ground up with the wheat, this can have unfortunate consequences. Writers about plants, from the Greeks Theophrastus and Dioscorides onwards, have warned us of the poisonous effects of darnel. It is said to cause blindness and drunkenness; Gerard in his *Herball* of 1597 talks of 'drunken darnel'—'the new bread wherein darnel is, eaten hot causeth drunkenness'.

Darnel grass is not only a nuisance in the Near East; it often infests wheat fields in England. Modern farmers would agree with our Lord's advice about how to tackle this problem—'Let both grow together until the harvest', and afterwards separate them.

THORNS and THISTLES

'Thorns *also and* thistles *shall it bring forth to thee; and thou shalt eat the herb of the field*' (Genesis 3:18).

This was God's punishment of Adam for eating of the forbidden fruit. Thorns and thistles (plate 30) are mentioned very often in the Bible and there is no sure way of identifying them. Adam's thorns and thistles may have been the spotted golden thistle *Scolymus maculatus*, or the star thistle, *Centaurea calcitrapa*, both frequent weeds in the hot and rocky regions of the Holy Land.

PLATE 28

The desert shall rejoice, and blossom as

the Rose.

ISAIAH. Chᵗ XXXV, PART ᴏꜰ VERSE I.

WHEAT *Triticum compositum (Gramineae)*

'... *gather the* wheat *into my barn*' (Matthew 13:30).

References to corn or grain, chaff and straw abound in the Bible. They are all cereals and were, all things considered, slightly more important than those other vital plants of the Holy Land—the grape vine and the olive tree.

The Hebrew for wheat is *chittah*. It is the main constituent of the 'corn' of the Bible which is mentioned over and over again. Palestine was known for the excellent quality of its wheat (plate 29); the main threat to it was drought, leading to famine—'*And there was a famine in the land: And Abram went down into Egypt to sojourn there; for the famine was grievous in the land*' (Genesis 12:10). Later, when the country became more settled from, say, the reign of Solomon onwards, and the Israelites had stopped wandering, the land produced regular bumper crops of wheat and Palestine became an exporter of grain, which was carried over the seas in the ships of her rich and powerful neighbour Tyre. '*Judah, and the land of Israel, they were thy merchants: they traded in thy market* wheat ... *and honey, and oil, and balm*' (Ezekiel 27:17).

Methods of cultivation have not changed much since the days of Isaiah. Wheat is still 'trodden out' by oxen or threshed with a flail and then winnowed with a fan and sifters. The period of the wheat harvest is today as it was then the main division of the year. The harvest generally takes place in June, when the wheat is cut down with sharp sickles.

YELLOW FLAG *Iris pseudacorus (Iridaceae)*

'... *and she laid it in the* flags *by the river's brink*' (Exodus 2:3).

'*Can the rush grow up without mire? can the* flag *grow without water?*' asked Job rhetorically (Job 8:11). The yellow flag iris (plate 8) certainly flourishes on wet marshy ground. It grows in shallow water on the edges of ponds and streams. The flowers are a deep yellow. It is not a Palestinian plant. Other types of iris, however, such as *Iris nazarena* (Nazareth iris) and *Iris costeti* (Costet's iris), provide some of the loveliest sights of Galilee in the early spring.

Gather ye together first the Tares, & bind them in bundles to burn them: but gather the Wheat into my barn.

MAT. Ch XIII. part of. V ER. XXX.

Every mention of each plant in the Old and New Testament is given in the list of references with the exception of certain plants which occur repeatedly. In these cases—the olive, vine, fig, thorn and thistle—we have included only a few sample references to each; otherwise the list would be ridiculously long.

REFERENCES

Aloe
Psalms 45:8
Proverbs 7:17
Song of Solomon 4:14
John 19:39

Almond
Genesis 28:19
30:37
35:6
43:11
Exodus 25:33–36
37:19–20
Numbers 17:1–8
Joshua 16:2
18:13
Ecclesiastes 12:5
Jeremiah 1:11

Apples (of gold)
Genesis 2:9, 17
3:6
Proverbs 25:11
Song of Solomon 2:3, 5
7:8
8:5
Joel 1:12

Aspalanthus
Ecclesiastes 24:15

Balm (balsam)
Genesis 37:25
Jeremiah 8:22
46:11
51:8
Ezekiel 27:17

Barley
Exodus 9:31
Deuteronomy 8:8
Judges 7:13
I Kings 4:28

Bay tree
Psalms 37:35

Beans
II Samuel 17:27–28
Ezekiel 4:9

Box
Isaiah 41:19
60:13

Brambles
Numbers 33:55
Luke 6:44

Briers
Judges 8:7, 16
Isaiah 7:23–25
9:18
10:17
55:13
Micah 7:4
Luke 6:44
Hebrews 6:8

Bulrush
Exodus 2:3, 5
Job 8:11
Isaiah 18:2
19:6–7
35:7
58:5

Camphire
Song of Solomon 1:14
4:13

Cassia
Exodus 30:23–24
Psalms 45:8
Ezekiel 27:19

Cedar
Judges 9:15
I Kings 4:33
Psalms 29:5
Isaiah 41:19
Amos 2:9

Chestnut
Genesis 30:37
Ezekiel 31:8
Ecclesiasticus 24:14

Cinnamon
Exodus 30:23
Proverbs 7:17
Song of Solomon 4:14
Revelation 18:13

Cockle
Job 31:40

Coriander
Exodus 16:31
Numbers 11:7

Cucumber
Numbers 11:5
Isaiah 1:8

Cypress
Ecclesiasticus 24:13
50:10

Ebony
Ezekiel 27:15

Fig tree
Genesis 3:7
I Samuel 25:18
Matthew 21:1, 19–21
24:32
Mark 11:13, 20
Luke 6:44
13:6–9

Fitches
Isaiah 28:25, 27

Flax
Exodus 9:31
Joshua 2:6
Judges 15:14
Isaiah 19:9
42:3
Hosea 2:5, 9
Matthew 12:20

Fuller's soap
Jeremiah 2:22
Malachi 3:2
Susannah 17

Garlic
Numbers 11:5

Grape-vine
Genesis 9:20–21, 24
Exodus 22:5
Leviticus 19:10
Numbers 13:20, 23–24
Deuteronomy 8:8
Psalms 78:47
Song of Solomon 1:14
Isaiah 1:8
Matthew 21:33
26:27–29
Mark 12:1
Luke 20:9–16
John 15:1–6
Revelation 14:18–20

Hazel
Genesis 30:37

Heath
Jeremiah 17:5–6

Hemlock
Hosea 10:4
Amos 6:12

Hyssop
Exodus 12:22
Leviticus 14:4, 6, 22
Numbers 19:6, 18
I Kings 4:33
Psalms 51:7
Hebrews 9:19

Ivy
II Maccabees 6:7

Juniper
I Kings 19:4–5
Psalms 120:4

Leeks
Numbers 11:5

Lentil
Genesis 25:34
II Samuel 17:27–29
23:11
I Chronicles 11:13
Ezekiel 4:9

Lily of the field
Matthew 6:28–30
Luke 12:27–28

Lily of the valley
Song of Solomon 2:1–2, 16
4:5
6:2–4

Mallows
Job 30:4

Mandrake
Genesis 30:14–16
Song of Solomon 7:13

Melon
Numbers 11:5

PLATE 30

Thorns also and Thistles shall it bring forth to thee.

GENESIS. Ch III, Ver XVIII.

BIBLIOGRAPHY

Balfour, J. H., *The Plants of the Bible*, 1885
Crowfoot, G. M. and L. Baldensperger, *From Cedar to Hyssop: a Study in the Folklore of Plants in Palestine*, 1904
Hepper, Nigel, *Bible Plants at Kew*, 1979
Moldenke, H. N. & A. L. E., *Plants of the Bible*, 1952
Temple, Augusta, *Flowers and Trees of Palestine*, 1907